First World War
and Army of Occupation
War Diary
France, Belgium and Germany

60 DIVISION
Divisional Troops
Royal Army Veterinary Corps
2/2 London Mobile Veterinary Section
26 June 1916 - 30 November 1916

WO95/3029/7

The Naval & Military Press Ltd
www.nmarchive.com
Published in association with The National Archives

Published by

The Naval & Military Press Ltd

Unit 10 Ridgewood Industrial Park,

Uckfield, East Sussex,

TN22 5QE England

Tel: +44 (0) 1825 749494

www.naval-military-press.com

www.nmarchive.com

This diary has been reprinted in facsimile from the original. Any imperfections are inevitably reproduced and the quality may fall short of modern type and cartographic standards.

© **Crown Copyright**
Images reproduced by permission of The National Archives, London, England, 2015.

Contents

Document type	Place/Title	Date From	Date To
Heading	WO95/3029/6		
Heading	60th Division 2-2nd London Mobile Vety Secn Jun-Nov 1916		
Heading	War Diary of Intelligence Summary Of 2/2nd London Mobile Veterinary Section (60th Division) Vol 1		
War Diary	Havre	26/06/1916	26/06/1916
War Diary	Petit Houvin (Sq A21. Mp.)	27/06/1916	27/06/1916
War Diary	Flers	27/06/1916	27/06/1916
War Diary	Villers Chatel (Sq.v.18 M.d)	28/06/1916	30/06/1916
Heading	War Diary of Intelligence Summary Of 2/2nd London Mobile Veterinary Section (60th Division) Vol II		
War Diary	Villers Chatel (Sq. V.18.M.D)	01/07/1916	14/07/1916
War Diary	La Mon Rouge Aubigny (Sq D18.M.A)	15/07/1916	31/07/1916
Heading	War Diary of Intelligence Summary Of 2/2nd London Mobile Veterinary Section Y.F. 60th London Division Vol III		
War Diary	La Mon Rouge Aubigny	01/08/1916	31/08/1916
Heading	War Diary of Intelligence Summary Of 2/2nd London Mobile Veterinary Section 60th London Division September 1916 Vol 4		
War Diary	La Mon Rouge Aubigny	01/09/1916	30/09/1916
Heading	War Diary of 60 London Mobile Veterinary Section 60th London Division October 1916 Vol 5		
War Diary	La Mon Rouce Aubigny	01/10/1916	31/10/1916
War Diary	Bernaville	01/11/1916	02/11/1916
War Diary	Famachon	03/11/1916	13/11/1916
War Diary	Longpre	14/11/1916	16/11/1916
War Diary	Marseilles	17/11/1916	30/11/1916

WO 95/3029/6

60TH DIVISION

2-2ND LONDON MOBILE VETY SECN

JUN-NOV 1916

June 1916.

Vol 1

War Diary
of
Intelligence Summary
of
2nd London Mobile Veterinary Section.
(60th Division.)

Army Form C. 2118.

WAR DIARY
or
INTELLIGENCE SUMMARY

(Erase heading not required.)

Instructions regarding War Diaries and Intelligence Summaries are contained in F. S. Regs., Part II. and the Staff Manual respectively. Title Pages will be prepared in manuscript.

Place	Date	Hour	Summary of Events and Information	Remarks and references to Appendices
HAVRE.	26.6.16	5.15 A.M.	Arrived HAVRE. (S.S. NORTHWESTERN MILLER. No. 3021.)	
		6.0 A.M.	Disembarked and proceeded to No.1. Rest Camp.	
	26.6.16	8.0 A.M.	Marched to HAVRE Railway Station. Horses and men entrained. Iron rations drawn.	
PETIT HOUVIN (Sq. A.D. M.D.)	27.6.16	5.0 A.M.	Detrained and proceeded to FLERS. Horse of Royal Engineers injured during journey, healed and left in care of local mayor. PETIT HOUVIN.	
FLERS.	27.6.16.	6.0 A.M.	Arrived FLERS. Horse lines erected. Men billeted.	
VILLERS CHATEL (Sq. V.S. M.D.)	28.6.16	8.0 A.M.	Proceeded by route march to VILLERS CHATEL. Halted at MAIZIERES. (Sq. C.25. M.B.) horses watered and fed.	
		4.0 P.M.	Arrived VILLERS CHATEL.	
	29.6.16.		Cleaned and examined picketing area for reception of sick horses.	
	30.6.16.		Visited horses left by units with local mayors at MONTS-EN-TERNOIS (Sq.B.26.M.D.) and GOUY-EN-TERNOIS (Sq.H.5.M.A.)	

H. Lane Lobb
A.D.V.S.
60TH DIVISION.

J.R.Beckett
Capt. A.V.C.
O.C. 2nd Jom. Mobile Veterinary Section

July 1916.

Secret

Vol II

War Diary
or
Intelligence Summary.
of
2nd London Mobile Veterinary Section.
(60th Division.)

Army Form C. 2118.

WAR DIARY
or
INTELLIGENCE SUMMARY
(Erase heading not required.)

Instructions regarding War Diaries and Intelligence Summaries are contained in F. S. Regs., Part II. and the Staff Manual respectively. Title Pages will be prepared in manuscript.

Place	Date	Hour	Summary of Events and Information	Remarks and references to Appendices
VILLERS CHATEL (Sq.V.15. M.D.)	1.7.16		Visited horses left by Units with Local Mayors at MAIZIERES. (Sq.C.25. M.B.) and VILLERS BRULIN (Sq.V.27. M.A.) Injuries dressed.	
	2.7.16		Collected nine horses of 60th Division left with 9/ot Mobile Veterinary Section. 51st Division at La Mon Rouge - AUBIGNY. (Sq.D.8. M.A.) Visited horse of Royal Engineers left at PETIT HOUVIN. (Sq.A.21.M.D.) Dressed injury. Three horses admitted for treatment.	
	3.7.16.		Collected horse from Local Maire BETHONSART. (Sq.V.15. M.D.) Destroyed horse with broken leg. of 2/3rd Batn. London Regt. at SAVY. (Sq.D.5. M.C.) Six horses admitted for treatment.	
	4.7.16		Proceeded to SAVY (Sq.D.5. M.C.) to see if horse destroyed 3.7.16 had been properly buried. One horse admitted for treatment.	
	5.7.16.		Inspected all horses of Royal Engineers stationed at VILLERS CHATEL. (Sq.V.15. M.D.) Inoculated with MALLEIN horses on strength of Mobile Veterinary Section. Visited horses left by Units with Local Mayors at MONTS-EN-TERNOIS. (Sq.B.26. M.B.) and GOUY-EN-TERNOIS. (Sq.H.5. M.A.) One horse admitted for treatment.	
	6.7.16.		Visited horse of Royal Engineers left at PETIT HOUVIN (Sq.A.21. M.D.) Dressed injury. Three horses admitted for treatment.	
	7.7.16		Visited three horses left by Units at CHELERS (Sq.U.22. M.B.) Dressed injuries. One horse admitted for treatment.	
	8.7.16		Inspected all horses of Royal Engineers at VILLERS CHATEL. (Sq.V.8. M.D.) One horse admitted for treatment.	
	9.7.16.		Visited horses left by Units at ST. MICHEL-SUR-TERNOISE (Sq.S.18. M.D.) Dressed injuries. " " " " " MINGOVAL (Sq.V.33. M.D.) Dressed injuries One horse admitted for treatment.	

H.Beckett Capt. A.V.C.
OC 2nd Lowland Mobile Veterinary Section

WAR DIARY
or
INTELLIGENCE SUMMARY

(Erase heading not required.)

Army Form C. 2118.

Place	Date	Hour	Summary of Events and Information	Remarks and references to Appendices
VILLERS CHATEL (Sq. V15. M.D.)	10.7.16		Visited all Royal Engineer horses at VILLERS CHATEL. Visited horse of Royal Engineers left at PETIT HOUVIN. (Sq. A21. M.D.) Diseased injuries.	
	11.7.16		The work done during this week comprises:— Three horses admitted for treatment. Treatment of horses unable to work and left by Units with Local Mayors pending receipt of horse float. Collection of horses from Units etc. for treatment.	
			One horse admitted for treatment.	
	12.7.16		Visited Royal Engineer horses at Villers Chatel. One horse admitted for treatment. One horse discharged, cured.	
	13.7.16		Party conducted four sick horses to Veterinary Hospital, Abbeville. Visited horse of Royal Engineers at PETIT HOUVIN. (Sq. A21. M.D.)	
	14.7.16		Collected horse from SAVY (Sq. D5.M.C.)	
LA MON ROUGE AUBIGNY (Sq. D15. M.A.)	15.7.16		Proceeded to new station at LA MON ROUGE AUBIGNY. Six horses admitted for treatment.	
	16.7.16		Took charge of Isolation Boxes at AUBIGNY. (Sq. E7. M.D.) Disinfected & cleaned new quarters. Buried dead horse. Picketing posts, lines etc., erected.	
	17.7.16		Collected sick horse from Berles (Sq. D14.M.B.) and ACQ (Sq. E12.M.C.) Six horses admitted from Units for treatment.	
			The work done during this week comprises:— 14 horses admitted for treatment. Examination of animals in charge of Royal Engineers. Evacuation of four horses to Veterinary Hospital. Taking over and preparing new quarters. The supervision of sick horses isolated, and treatment of 17 horses remaining on Veterinary Section Lines.	Capt. A.P.V. A.W. Beckett O/C Mobile Veterinary Section.

2449 Wt. W14957/M90 750,000 1/16 J.B.C. & A. Forms/C.2118/12.

Army Form C. 2118.

WAR DIARY
or
INTELLIGENCE SUMMARY
(Erase heading not required.)

Instructions regarding War Diaries and Intelligence Summaries are contained in F.S. Regs., Part II and the Staff Manual respectively. Title Pages will be prepared in manuscript.

Place	Date	Hour	Summary of Events and Information	Remarks and references to Appendices
LA MON ROUGE AUBIGNY. (S.D. 18. M.a.)	18.7.16		Collected two horses from GAMBLIGNEUL. (Sg. W1.H. M.D.) Eleven horses admitted for treatment.	
	19.7.16		Party conducted 17 horses to Veterinary Hospital, ABBEVILLE. One horse admitted for treatment.	
	20.7.16		Collected timber for erecting pickets and lines from MAROEUIL (Sg. F.27. M.a.) Admitted 5 horses and four mules.	
	21.7.16		Erected additional picketing posts and lines. Collected horse from FREVIN CAPELLE. (Sg. E.10. M.a.) Admitted 14 horses and 3 mules. One horse discharged.	
	22.7.16		Visited horse of Royal Engineers left at PETIT HOUVIN (Sg. A.21. M.3.) Dressed injuries. Admitted 7 horses and one mule.	
	23.7.16		Party conducted 16 horses and 5 mules to Veterinary Hospital, ABBEVILLE. Two men detailed for duty at Isolation Boxes, to replace men of 31st D.A.C. returned to Unit. Admitted 2 horses and one mule.	
	24.7.16		One N.C.O. and A.S.C. Driver detailed for ABBEVILLE (by road) with limbered waggon to exchange for sick horse float. Collected horse from A.C.Q. (Sg. E.12. M.C.) Admitted 14 horses for treatment and 9 horses in errors of Units' Establishments.	
			The work done during the week comprised :- Collection of four horses from Units. Admission of 54 horses and 9 mules for treatment. Reception of 9 horses left by various Units in errors of Establishment - return of these to other Units. Evacuation of 33 horses and 5 mules to Veterinary Hospital.	

H. Beckett Captain R.A.V.C.
O.C. #4 London Mobile Veterinary Section

2449 Wt. W14957/M90 750,000 1/16 J.B.C. & A. Forms/C.2118/12.

WAR DIARY
or
INTELLIGENCE SUMMARY

Army Form C. 2118.

Place	Date	Hour	Summary of Events and Information	Remarks and references to Appendices
LA MÔN ROUGE AUBIGNY. (Sq. D18. M.a.)	25.7.16		Collected 2 horses from BERLES. (Sq. D10. M.4.) Discharged nine horses cured. Admitted three horses for treatment and two horses in excess of Units' establishments	
	26.7.16		Collected six horses from Local Mayor, St. MICHEL-SUR-TERNOIS. (Sq. S18. M.D.) Party conducted 9 horses and one mule to Veterinary Hospital. ABBEVILLE Three horses discharged cured. Eleven horses admitted for treatment.	
"	27.7.16		Party conducted 21 horses to Veterinary Hospital. ABBEVILLE One horse and one mule admitted Sealed horse at Bray (3/4th Batn. London Regt.) Sq. F20. M.b.	
"	28.7.16.		Eight horses admitted for treatment, and three horses in excess of Units' Establishment. Two horses discharged cured. Horse float arrived from ABBEVILLE (by road.)	
"	29.7.16		Two horses admitted for treatment. Horse collected by float from St MICHEL-SUR-TERNOISE. (Sq 518. M.D.) " " " " FREVIN CAPELLE. (Sq. E10. M.A.)	
"	30.7.16.		Party conducted 13 horses and one mule to Veterinary Hospital. ABBEVILLE Twelve horses discharged cured. Three horses admitted for treatment. (Sq. D18. M.3.) Collected horse from BERLES by float. (Sq. D18. M.3.) Remounts detrained AUBIGNY Railway Station. (Sq. E7.M.a.) taken to Mobile Veterinary Section lines and issued from there.	
"	31.7.16.		Collected horse by float from BRAY (Sq. F20. M.b.) " " " " " BERLES. (Sq. D18. M.4.) Five horses admitted for treatment.	

The work done during the week comprises:- Collection of horses unable to walk by float. Admission of 33 horses for treatment and evacuation. Evacuation of 43 horses and 2 mules to Veterinary Hospital. Issue of cured and surplus horses. Unloading and issue of Remounts for Units of 60th Division.

J.H. Beckett Lieut.
R.A.V.C. Asst. Assistant Veterinary Section

A.D.V.S.
60TH DIVISION.

August 1916.

Vol III

War Diary
or
Intelligence Summary
of
2nd London Mobile Veterinary Section T.F.
60th London Division

WAR DIARY or INTELLIGENCE SUMMARY

Army Form C. 2118.

(Erase heading not required.)

Mobile Veterinary Section
60th (LONDON DIVISION)

Place	Date	Hour	Summary of Events and Information	Remarks and references to Appendices
LA MON ROUGE AUBIGNY.	1.8.16		Inspected horses of Hants. Cavalry Yeomanry and Yorkshire Hussars BERLES. Admitted five/ol horses for treatment and evacuation to No.22 Veterinary Hospital ABBEVILLE.	
	2.8.16		Visited horse of Royal Engineers left at PETIT HOUVIN. Prepared documents for evacuation of horses to Veterinary Hospital. Collected 8 N.D. Horses from Field Remount Section GOUY-EN-TERNOIS.	
	3.8.16.		Inspected horses of 21st Reserve Park BERLES. Admitted six horses for treatment and evacuation to Base Veterinary Hospital. Daily conducts twelve horses to No.22 Veterinary Hospital ABBEVILLE. Collected disabled horse by foot from M.V.P. MAROEUIL. Inspected horses of 230th Army Troops and 17th Corps Cyclist Coy. AUBIGNY. Admitted seven horses and six mules for treatment and evacuation. Prepared papers for evacuation of horses to Base Veterinary Hospital. Two horses discharged cured. Collected by foot disabled horses from BERLES.	
	4.8.16		Twenty three horses and six mules evacuated to No.22 Veterinary Hospital ABBEVILLE. Visited horses of Hants Berkshire Yeomanry BERLES. Four horses admitted for treatment.	
	5.8.16.-		Collected disabled horse by foot from 1st Essex R.F.A. HABARCQ WOOD. Three horses admitted for treatment. Inspected horses of Yorkshire Hussars, BERLES.	
			The work done this week comprises:- Daily visits to Isolation Shed, AUBIGNY. Veterinary care of horses of Hants Cavalry and Yorkshire Hussars. Admission and treatment of 55 horses and 12 mules. Evacuation to Veterinary Hospital ABBEVILLE of 46 horses and 6 mules. Collection and treatment of disabled horses.	Beckett Capt. O i/c M.V.S.

2449 Wt. W14957/M90 750,000 1/16 J.B.C. & A. Forms/C.2118/12.

Army Form C. 2118.

WAR DIARY
or
INTELLIGENCE SUMMARY

(Erase heading not required.)

Instructions regarding War Diaries and Intelligence Summaries are contained in F. S. Regs., Part II. and the Staff Manual respectively. Title Pages will be prepared in manuscript.

Place	Date	Hour	Summary of Events and Information	Remarks and references to Appendices
LA MONROUGE AUBIGNY.	6.8.16.		Sixteen horses evacuated to No.22 Veterinary Hospital, ABBEVILLE. Six horses issued to Units of Division. Two horses discharged cured. One horse admitted for treatment. Horse of Royal Engineers collected from PETIT HOUVIN and returned to Unit.	
	7.8.16.		Four horses admitted for treatment. Two horses issued cured.	
	8.8.16.		Three horses admitted for treatment. Two horses returned cured.	
	9.8.16.		Three horses admitted for treatment. Thirteen N.D. horses collected from 2nd. Division, DUISANS. Six horses issued to Units. Six horses and two mules evacuated to No.22 Veterinary Hospital, ABBEVILLE.	
	10.8.16		Eleven horses and five mules admitted for treatment.	
	11.8.16		Eleven horses and six mules evacuated to No.22 Veterinary Hospital, ABBEVILLE. Three horses admitted for treatment. Disabled horse collected by float from Artillery at ACQ. Two horses discharged.	
	12.8.16.		Four horses admitted for treatment. One horse discharged.	
			The work done during the week comprises:- Admission and treatment of 29 horses and five mules. Evacuation to Base Veterinary Hospital, 33 horses and eight mules. Collection and treatment of disabled horse. Collection and issue N.D. Horses from Duisans. Daily visits to Isolation sheds AUBIGNY.	

J.B. Beckett Cpl
No. 72 L.m.V.S.

Army Form C. 2118.

WAR DIARY
or
INTELLIGENCE SUMMARY
(Erase heading not required.)

Instructions regarding War Diaries and Intelligence Summaries are contained in F. S. Regs., Part II and the Staff Manual respectively. Title Pages will be prepared in manuscript.

Place	Date	Hour	Summary of Events and Information	Remarks and references to Appendices
LA MAISON ROUGE AUBIGNY.	13.8.16		Seven horses admitted for treatment.	
	14.8.16		Eight horses admitted for treatment.	
	15.8.16		Eight horses admitted for treatment. Eleven horses and four mules evacuated to No. 22. Veterinary Hospital ABBEVILLE. Two horses discharged.	
	16.8.16		Four horses admitted for treatment. Two horses discharged.	
	17.8.16		Remounts detrained AUBIGNY Railway Station, taken to Mobile Veterinary Section lines & issued from there. Eight horses admitted for treatment. Eight horses evacuated to No. 22 Veterinary Hospital ABBEVILLE.	
	18.8.16		Seven horses and one mule evacuated to No. 22 Veterinary Hospital ABBEVILLE. Three horses admitted for treatment. One horse discharged.	
	19.8.16		Two horses and six mules admitted for treatment. Two mules discharged. Disabled mule collected by Motor Lorry from FREVIN CAPELLE.	

The work done during this week comprises:-

Admission and treatment of 43 horses and 7 mules.
Evacuation to Base Veterinary Hospital, 11 horses and 7 mules.
Daily visits to Isolation Sheds, AUBIGNY.
Unloading Remounts AUBIGNY Railway Station and issue from Mobile Veterinary Section Lines.

JB Beckett Capt
O/c 2 L.M.V.S.

Army Form C. 2118.

WAR DIARY
or
INTELLIGENCE SUMMARY
(Erase heading not required.)

Instructions regarding War Diaries and Intelligence Summaries are contained in F. S. Regs., Part II. and the Staff Manual respectively. Title Pages will be prepared in manuscript.

Place	Date	Hour	Summary of Events and Information	Remarks and references to Appendices
LA MAISON ROUGE AUBIGNY.	20.8.16		Five horses and three mules evacuated to No. 22 Veterinary Hospital. ABBEVILLE. Eight horses admitted for treatment. Disabled horse collected from Artillery at ACQ.	
	21.8.16		Nineteen horses admitted for treatment. Disabled mule collected from 179th Machine Gun Coy. One horse discharged.	
	22.8.16		Stray horse admitted. Horse standings commenced for approaching winter. Existing stabling strengthened.	
	23.8.16		Twenty two horses and four mules evacuated to No. 22. Veterinary Hospital. ABBEVILLE One horse admitted for treatment.	
	24.8.16		Fifteen horses admitted for treatment. Work continued on horse standings.	
	25.8.16		Six horses admitted for treatment. Six surplus horses admitted - for evacn. Work continued on winter horse standings. One horse discharged.	
	26.8.16		Fourteen horses and five mules evacuated to No. 22 Veterinary Hospital. ABBEVILLE. Fourteen horses admitted for treatment. Stray horse admitted 22.8.16 claimed by Artillery. Two horses discharged. Winter horse standings continued.	
			The work done during this week comprises. Admission for treatment of 49 horses. Evacuation of 41 horses and 12 mules. Collection & treatment of disabled horses. Admission & receival of surplus horses. Making good existing stabling and preparing standings for approaching winter. Daily visits to isolation area, AUBIGNY.	J.B. Prokett? Capt O i/c 2 MVS

2449 Wt. W14957/M90 750,000 1/16 J.B.C. & A. Forms/C.2118/12.

WAR DIARY
INTELLIGENCE SUMMARY

Army Form C. 2118.

Place	Date	Hour	Summary of Events and Information	Remarks and references to Appendices
LA MON ROUGE AUBIGNY.	27.8.16		Disabled horse collected by Mot. from Artillery at ACQ. Sixl surplus horses admitted for removal. Three horses issued.	
	28.8.16		Disabled horse collected by float from Yorks Hussars. BERLES. Sixteen horses evacuated to No. 12 Veterinary Hospital. ABBEVILLE. Sick horses issued to Units. Work continued on horse standings.	
	29.8.16		Thirteen horses admitted for treatment. Nineteen surplus horses admitted - for removal. One M.D. horse collected by float from HABARCQ WOOD. Work continued on horse standings.	
	30.8.16		Nine surplus admitted for removal. Work continued on horse standings.	
	31.8.16		Twenty two horses and two mules evacuated to No. 22 Veterinary Hospital ABBEVILLE. Work continued on horse standings.	Daily visits to Isolation sheds, AUBIGNY. Collection & treatment of disabled horses.
HY. FOOD		17.01	The work done during this week comprises:- Daily visits to Isolation Boxes, AUBIGNY. Evacuation of 38 horses and two mules. Admission & treatment of thirteen horses. Admission of 33 surplus horses for removal. Issue of surplus horses.	

A.D.V.S.
60TH DIVISION.

A. Beckett. Capt. A.V.C.
O.C. 2nd/Lon. Mobile Veterinary Section.

September 1916.

Vol 4

War Diary
or
Intelligence Summary
of
2nd London Mobile Veterinary Section
60th London Division.

Army Form C. 2118.

WAR DIARY
or
INTELLIGENCE SUMMARY

(Erase heading not required.)

Instructions regarding War Diaries and Intelligence Summaries are contained in F. S. Regs., Part II and the Staff Manual respectively. Title Pages will be prepared in manuscript.

Place	Date	Hour	Summary of Events and Information	Remarks and references to Appendices
LA MON ROUGE AUBIGNY	1.9.16.		Two horses and one mule admitted for treatment. Six horses and one mule sent to No. 22 Veterinary Hospital. ABBEVILLE. One horse found by 2/20th Battalion London Regiment, admitted. Three horses discharged.	
	2.9.16.		Six horses admitted for treatment. Eight horses sent to No. 22 Veterinary Hospital ABBEVILLE. Disabled horse collected by float from Headquarters, 60th Division. HERMAVILLE. One horse discharged.	
	3.9.16.		Fifteen horses and one mule admitted for treatment. Disabled horse collected by float from Artillery at ACQ. One hundred and thirty five surplus Artillery horses admitted.	
	4.9.16.		Five horses admitted for treatment. Sixteen horses sent to No. 22 Veterinary Hospital. ABBEVILLE. Forty surplus Artillery horses sent Remount Depot. ABBEVILLE.	
	5.9.16.		Eight horses and five mules admitted for treatment. Three horses discharged.	
	6.9.16.		Eight horses and one mule admitted for treatment. Two horses found by 2/21st Battalion London Regiment admitted. Twelve horses and four mules sent to No. 22 Veterinary Hospital. ABBEVILLE. Forty seven surplus Artillery horses sent Remount Depot. ABBEVILLE.	
	7.9.16.		Three horses and three mules admitted for treatment. Seven horses and one mule sent to No. 22 Veterinary Hospital. ABBEVILLE. Two horses found 6.9.16. claimed by Artillery.	

A. Beckett Capt.

2449 Wt. W14957/M90 750,000 1/16 J.B.C. & A. Forms/C.2118/12.

Army Form C. 2118.

WAR DIARY
or
INTELLIGENCE SUMMARY

(Erase heading not required.)

Instructions regarding War Diaries and Intelligence Summaries are contained in F. S. Regs., Part II. and the Staff Manual respectively. Title Pages will be prepared in manuscript.

Place	Date	Hour	Summary of Events and Information	Remarks and references to Appendices
La Mon Rouge Aubigny.	8.9.16.		Five horses admitted for treatment. Two horses discharged.	
	9.9.16.		Four horses admitted for treatment. Ten horses and four mules sent to No. 22 Veterinary Hospital. ABBEVILLE. Disabled horses collected by float from 180th Machine Gun Co. BRAY. The work done during this week comprises:— Admission and treatment of 48 horses and 6 mules. Evacuation to Base Veterinary Hospital 69 horses and 10 mules. Collection & treatment of disabled horses. Supervision of horses at Isolation Boxes AUBIGNY.— Daily visits. One hundred and thirty three surplus Artillery horses admitted. Evacuation to Remount Depôt. ABBEVILLE — 87 Surplus Artillery horses. Work continued on winter horse standings.	
	10.9.16.		Ten horses admitted for treatment. Fifteen horses and one mule sent No. 22 Veterinary Hospital. ABBEVILLE.	
	11.9.16.		Two horses admitted for treatment. Two horses discharged.	
	12.9.16.		Eleven horses and two mules admitted for treatment. Disabled horses collected by float from HAUTE AVESNES. Ten horses and two mules sent No. 22 Veterinary Hospital. ABBEVILLE.	

A.B.Ackett Capt

Army Form C. 2118.

WAR DIARY
or
INTELLIGENCE SUMMARY

(Erase heading not required.)

Instructions regarding War Diaries and Intelligence Summaries are contained in F.S. Regs., Part II. and the Staff Manual respectively. Title Pages will be prepared in manuscript.

Place	Date	Hour	Summary of Events and Information	Remarks and references to Appendices
LA MON ROUGE AUGIGNY.	13.9.16		Seven horses admitted for treatment. Disabled horse collected by float from Artillery at ACQ. Four horses discharged.	
	14.9.16.		One horse admitted for treatment. Eight horses evacuated to No 22 Veterinary Hospital, ABBEVILLE.	
	15.9.16.		Five horses and one mule admitted for treatment. Stray horse admitted. Two horses discharged.	
	16.9.16.		Seven horses and four mules admitted for treatment. Seven horses and one mule evacuated to No 22 Veterinary Hospital ABBEVILLE. Two horses discharged. Disabled horse collected by float from RAUCOURT-EN-LEAX. The work done during this week comprises:- Admission & treatment of 43 horses and 7 mules. Evacuation of 40 horses and 4 mules. Collection & treatment of disabled horses. Daily visits to Isolation Sheds. AUGIGNY. Work continued on whole horse standing.	
	17.9.16		Disabled horse collected by float from Artillery at LARRASSET. Ten horses and four mules evacuated to Veterinary Hospital. ABBEVILLE.	
	18.9.16.		Three horses admitted for treatment. Disabled horse collected by float from PENIN. Three horses evacuated to No 22 Veterinary Hospital. ABBEVILLE.	

A.B. Beckett Capt.

Army Form C. 2118.

WAR DIARY
or
INTELLIGENCE SUMMARY

(Erase heading not required.)

Instructions regarding War Diaries and Intelligence Summaries are contained in F. S. Regs., Part II. and the Staff Manual respectively. Title Pages will be prepared in manuscript.

Place	Date	Hour	Summary of Events and Information	Remarks and references to Appendices
LA MAISON ROUGE AUBIGNY.	19.9.16.		Two horses admitted for treatment. Disabled horse collected by Boat from Mal. Front R.G.A. HABARCQ WOOD. Remounts unloaded AUBIGNY Station to bow to Mobile Veterinary Section lines and turned. Five horses Evacuated to No. 22 Veterinary Hospital. ABBEVILLE.	
	20.9.16		Five horses admitted for treatment. Three horses discharged.	
	21.9.16.		Four horses and one mule Evacuated to No. 22 Veterinary Hospital. ABBEVILLE. Three horses admitted for treatment.	
	22.9.16		Five horses and one mule admitted for treatment. Disabled mule collected by float from TREVIN CAPELLE.	
	23.9.16		Seven horses and two mules Evacuated to No. 22 Veterinary Hospital, ABBEVILLE. The work done during the week comprises: — Admission and treatment of 26 horses and 4 mules. Evacuation of 34 horses and 3 mules. Collection & treatment of disabled horses. Collection & issue of Remounts. Work continued on winter horse standings.	

J.P. Brickett Capt.

2449   Wt. W14957/M90 750,000 1/16 J.B.C. & A.   Forms/C.2118/12.

Army Form C. 2118.

WAR DIARY
or
INTELLIGENCE SUMMARY
(Erase heading not required.)

Instructions regarding War Diaries and Intelligence Summaries are contained in F.S. Regs., Part II and the Staff Manual respectively. Title Pages will be prepared in manuscript.

Place	Date	Hour	Summary of Events and Information	Remarks and references to Appendices
LA "ON ROUGE" AUBIGNY	24.9.16		Twenty six Remounts unloaded AUBIGNY Railway Station, taken to Mobile Veterinary Section Lines & issued. Eleven horses and one mule admitted for treatment. Thirteen horses and three mules evacuated to N°.22 Veterinary Hospital, ABBEVILLE. Two horses discharged.	
	25.9.16		Six horses and one mule evacuated to N°.22 Veterinary Hospital, ABBEVILLE.	
	26.9.16		Five horses and three mules admitted for treatment. Four horses and three mules evacuated to N°.22 Veterinary Hospital, ABBEVILLE.	
	27.9.16		Six horses and one mule admitted for treatment. Two horses discharged.	
	28.9.16		Seven horses and one mule evacuated to N°.22 Veterinary Hospital, ABBEVILLE. Two horses and one mule conducted by road to Remount Section FREVENT. Seven horses and one mule admitted for treatment.	
	29.9.16		Eight horses admitted for treatment. Two horses discharged. Eight horses evacuated to N°.22 Veterinary Hospital, ABBEVILLE. Two horses and one mule collected from Remount Section, FREVENT.	

JB Beckett Capt

Army Form C. 2118.

WAR DIARY
or
INTELLIGENCE SUMMARY
(Erase heading not required.)

Instructions regarding War Diaries and Intelligence Summaries are contained in F. S. Regs., Part II and the Staff Manual respectively. Title Pages will be prepared in manuscript.

Place	Date	Hour	Summary of Events and Information	Remarks and references to Appendices
LA MAISON ROUGE AUBIGNY	30.9.16		Four horses and one mule admitted for treatment. Five horses and two mules evacuated to No. 22 Veterinary Hospital ABBEVILLE. The work done during the week comprises:— Admission & treatment of 41 horses and 7 mules. Evacuation of 43 horses and 10 mules. Unloading, collection and distribution of Remounts. Work on Winter horse standings continued.	

A. Beckett Capt. A.V.C.
O/C 2/ndon. Mobile Veterinary Section.

A.D.V.S.
60TH DIVISION.

October 1916

Vol 5

War Diary —
of
60th London Mobile Veterinary Section
60th London Division

Army Form C. 2118.

WAR DIARY
or
INTELLIGENCE SUMMARY

(Erase heading not required.)

Instructions regarding War Diaries and Intelligence Summaries are contained in F. S. Regs., Part II. and the Staff Manual respectively. Title Pages will be prepared in manuscript.

Place	Date	Hour	Summary of Events and Information	Remarks and references to Appendices
LAMON ROUGE AUBIGNY.	1.10.16		Two horses discharged.	
	2.10.16		Two horses admitted. One horse discharged	
	3.10.16		Two horses admitted. Seven horses and one mule Evacuated to No 22 Veterinary Hospital. ABBEVILLE. Four horses issued.	
	4.10.16		Two horses admitted	
	5.10.16		Seven horses admitted. One horse issued	
	6.10.16		Ten horses and two mules admitted. Five horses evacuated to No 22 Veterinary Hospital. ABBEVILLE. Disabled horse collected by float from 146th Hvy Bty. R.G.A. HABARCQ WOOD	
	7.10.16		Five horses admitted One horse and one mule discharged. Eight horses Evacuated to No 22 Veterinary Hospital, ABBEVILLE. Two disabled horses collected by float from CONTEVILLE.	
			The work done during this week comprises:- Admission of 31 horses and 2 mules. Evacuation of 20 " " 1 " Discharged 9 " " 1 " Collection by float of Disabled Horses Work on winter horse standings	

2449 Wt. W14957/M90 750,000 1/16 J.B.C. & A. Forms/C.2118/12.

Army Form C. 2118.

WAR DIARY
or
INTELLIGENCE SUMMARY
(Erase heading not required.)

Instructions regarding War Diaries and Intelligence Summaries are contained in F. S. Regs., Part II. and the Staff Manual respectively. Title Pages will be prepared in manuscript.

Place	Date	Hour	Summary of Events and Information	Remarks and references to Appendices
La Mon Rouge	8.10.16		Two horses discharged.	
AUBIGNY	9.10.16		One horse admitted. One horse issued. One horse (disabled) collected by float from HAUTE AVESNES	
	10.10.16		Nine horses and two mules admitted. Eight horses evacuated to No. 22 Veterinary Hospital, ABBEVILLE. One horse issued. Two disabled horses collected by float — One from PENIN. One from OSTREVILLE	
	11.10.16		Two horses admitted. Seven horses evacuated to No. 22 Veterinary Hospital, ABBEVILLE. Three horses discharged. Six Surplus Artillery horses admitted — four issued.	
	12.10.16		Two horses admitted. Two disabled horses collected from PENIN and HAUTE AVESNES.	
	13.10.16		Five horses admitted. Disabled horse collected by float from Artillery at LARASSAT. Fifteen Remounts detrained AUBIGNY Station and taken to M.V.S Lines. Two Remounts issued.	
	14.10.16		Six horses and one mule evacuated to No 22 Veterinary Hospital, ABBEVILLE. Three horses admitted.	

2449 Wt. W14957/Mg0 750,000 1/16 J.B.C. & A. Forms/C.2118/12.

Army Form C. 2118.

WAR DIARY
or
INTELLIGENCE SUMMARY

(Erase heading not required.)

Place	Date	Hour	Summary of Events and Information	Remarks and references to Appendices
			The work done during this week comprises — Eleven horses discharged. Twenty one horses and one mule evacuated. Thirty one horses and two mules admitted. Collection of disabled horses. Collection and issue of Remounts. Work on winter horse standings.	

Army Form C. 2118.

WAR DIARY
or
INTELLIGENCE SUMMARY

(Erase heading not required.)

Instructions regarding War Diaries and Intelligence Summaries are contained in F. S. Regs., Part II. and the Staff Manual respectively. Title Pages will be prepared in manuscript.

Place	Date	Hour	Summary of Events and Information	Remarks and references to Appendices
LA MON ROUGE AUBIGNY	15.10.16		Four Remounts issued.	
	16.10.16		One horse discharged.	
	17.10.16		Disabled horse collected by float from HAUTE AVESNES	
	18.10.16		Five horses evacuated to No. 22 Veterinary Hospital ABBEVILLE. One horse admitted. Three Remounts issued. One horse collected by float from HERMAVILLE.	
	19.10.16		Three horses admitted. One horse collected by float from HERMAVILLE.	
	20.10.16		Twenty one horses and three mules admitted. Disabled horse collected by float from ACQ. Eight horses evacuated to No. 22 Veterinary Hospital ABBEVILLE.	
	21.10.16		Twelve horses and three mules admitted. Disabled horse collected by float from MAROEUIL. Eighteen horses and three mules evacuated to No. 22 Veterinary Hospital ABBEVILLE.	
			The work done during this week comprises - 40 horses and 6 mules admitted. 31 " " " evacuated. 5 " " 3 " discharged. Collection of disabled horses. Work on Winter horse standings.	

Army Form C. 2118.

WAR DIARY
or
INTELLIGENCE SUMMARY
(Erase heading not required.)

Instructions regarding War Diaries and Intelligence Summaries are contained in F. S. Regs., Part II. and the Staff Manual respectively. Title Pages will be prepared in manuscript.

Place	Date	Hour	Summary of Events and Information	Remarks and references to Appendices
LA MON ROUGE AUBIGNY.	22.10.16		Five horses and two mules admitted. Disabled horse collected from MONT ST ELOI. Eighteen horses and three mules Evacuated to No. 22 Veterinary Hospital ABBEVILLE.	
	23.10.16		Eight horses and five mules admitted. Disabled horses collected by float from MAROEUIL and ECOIVRES.	
	24.10.16		Two horses and one mule admitted. Disabled mule collected by float from MAROEUIL. Eleven horses and five mules Evacuated to No. 22 Veterinary Hospital. ABBEVILLE.	
	25.10.16		Five horses and three mules admitted. Two horses collected by float from ACQ. Remounts detained AUBIGNY Station, taken to M.V.S. Lines and cared from thes.	
	26.10.16		Six horses and five mules evacuated to No. 22 Veterinary Hospital, ABBEVILLE. Two horses admitted. Two horses collected by float from ACQ.	
	27.10.16		Moved by road to BROUILLY.	The work done during this week comprises:— Evacuated 35 horses and 13 mules, Admitted 22 " " 11 " Collection of disabled horses. Collection and issue of Remounts. Moved from AUBIGNY to BROUILLY and thence to FROHEN-LE-GRAND.
	28.10.16		Moved by road to FROHEN-LE-GRAND.	

Army Form C. 2118.

WAR DIARY
or
INTELLIGENCE SUMMARY

(Erase heading not required.)

Instructions regarding War Diaries and Intelligence Summaries are contained in F. S. Regs., Part II. and the Staff Manual respectively. Title Pages will be prepared in manuscript.

Place	Date	Hour	Summary of Events and Information	Remarks and references to Appendices
	29.10.16		Moved to BERNAVILLE, by road.	
	30.10.16		Horse lines cleaned and prepared for reception of R.O.R cases.	
	31.10.16		Two horses admitted.	

J.T Beckett
Capt. A.V.C.
O/C 60th London Mobile Veterinary Section

H.T. Leeen Lt Col.
A.D.V.S.
60TH DIVISION

2449 Wt. W14957/M90 750,000 1/16 J.B.C. & A. Forms/C.2118/12.

Army Form C. 2118.

2/60" Mobile Veterinary Section WAR DIARY November 1916.

INTELLIGENCE SUMMARY

Vol 6

(Erase heading not required.)

Instructions regarding War Diaries and Intelligence Summaries are contained in F. S. Regs., Part II. and the Staff Manual respectively. Title Pages will be prepared in manuscript.

Place	Date	Hour	Summary of Events and Information	Remarks and references to Appendices
BERNAVILLE	1.11.16		One horse admitted for cooking.	
	2.11.16		Two horses admitted for treatment	
FAMECHON	3.11.16		Proceeded by road march to FAMECHON.	
	4.11.16		Lines cleaned and preparations made for reception of sick animals	
	5.11.16			
	6.11.16		Three horses admitted for treatment	
	7.11.16		Six horses evacuated by road to No.22 Veterinary Hospital, ABBEVILLE. Seven horses and one mule admitted for treatment	
	8.11.16		Three horses admitted for treatment Two horses evacuated by road to No.22 Veterinary Hospital, ABBEVILLE.	
	9.11.16		Two horses admitted for treatment Seven horses evacuated by road to No.22 Veterinary Hospital, ABBEVILLE.	
	10.11.16		Two horses and one mule admitted for treatment	
	11.11.16		One horse and one mule admitted for treatment.	
	12.11.16		One horse admitted for treatment	

M Beckett. Capt. A.V.C.
for A.D.V.S.
60TH DIVISION.

Army Form C. 2118.

WAR DIARY
or
INTELLIGENCE SUMMARY
(Erase heading not required.)

Instructions regarding War Diaries and Intelligence Summaries are contained in F. S. Regs., Part II. and the Staff Manual respectively. Title Pages will be prepared in manuscript.

Place	Date	Hour	Summary of Events and Information	Remarks and references to Appendices
FANACHON.	13.11.16		One horse admitted for treatment.	
LONGPRE.	14.11.16		One half of Section proceeded by route march to LONGPRE Railway Station. - Entrained at 6.15 p.m.	
	15.11.16		Train journey continued.	
	16.11.16		Train journey continued.	
MARSEILLES	17.11.16		Arrived MARSEILLES. Proceeded to CAMP FOURNIER - arrived 1.30 a.m. Advanced Veterinary Hospital spätesten	
	18.11.16		Five horses admitted for treatment. All trains met with Veterinary shed and float.	
	19.11.16		Five horses and two mules admitted for treatment. - Veterinary shed and float met all trains.	
	20.11.16		Six horses and one mule admitted for treatment. - Veterinary shed and float met all trains.	
	21.11.16		Five horses admitted for treatment. - Veterinary shed and float met all trains.	
	22.11.16		Nine horses admitted for treatment. - Veterinary shed and float met all trains.	
	23.11.16		Five horses and one mule admitted for treatment. - Veterinary shed and float met all trains. Eight horses evacuated by road to Indian Veterinary Hospital. LA VALENTINE =	
	24.11.16		Three horses and one mule admitted for treatment. - Veterinary shed and float met all trains. Six horses (mange) evacuated by road to Indian Veterinary Hospital - LA VALENTINE. Two horses and one mule readmitted for treatment.	
	25.11.16		Remaining half Section arrived MARSEILLE.	
	26.11.16		One horse (stray) admitted for treatment.	

H. Beckett Capt. A.V.C.
for A.D.V.S.
60TH DIVISION.

Army Form C. 2118.

WAR DIARY
or
INTELLIGENCE SUMMARY

(Erase heading not required.)

Instructions regarding War Diaries and Intelligence Summaries are contained in F. S. Regs., Part II. and the Staff Manual respectively. Title Pages will be prepared in manuscript.

Place	Date	Hour	Summary of Events and Information	Remarks and references to Appendices
MARSEILLE	27.11.16		Four horses admitted for treatment.	
	28.11.16		Three horses and one mule admitted for treatment. Two horses returned to units, cured.	
	29.11.16		Two horses admitted for treatment.	
	30.11.16		Two horses admitted for treatment.	

F. Beckett Capt. A.V.C.
for A.D.V.S.
60TH DIVISION.

www.ingramcontent.com/pod-product-compliance
Lightning Source LLC
Chambersburg PA
CBHW081502160426
43193CB00014B/2562